Escape!

Written by Sharon Shavers Gayle

Illustrated by Eric Velasquez

Soundprints
Where Children Discover...

To my mother, Mamie, who not only taught me to read,
but also taught me that reading was the greatest shelter of all — S.S.G.

To the memory of all the courageous souls who freed themselves from slavery — E.V.

Illustrations copyright © 1999 Eric Velasquez
Book copyright © 1999 Trudy Corporation, 353 Main Avenue, Norwalk, CT 06851,
and the Smithsonian Institution, Washington, DC, 20560.

Soundprints is a division of Trudy Corporation, Norwalk, Connecticut.

Book Layout: Scott Findlay
Editor: Judy Gitenstein

First Edition 10 9 8 7 6 5 4 3 2 1
Printed in Hong Kong

Acknowledgments:
   Our thanks to Joanna Banks of the Smithsonian Institution's Anacostia Museum for her
curatorial review.

Library of Congress Cataloging-in-Publication Data

Gayle, Sharon Shavers
   Escape!: a story of the underground railroad / written by Sharon Shavers Gayle; illustrated by
Eric Velasquez.—1st ed.
          p.   cm.
   Summary: While on a visit to the Anacostia Museum of the Smithsonian Institution, Emma finds
herself as a runaway slave using the Underground Railroad to make her way to freedom in Canada.
   ISBN 1-56899-622-5 (hardcover)   ISBN 1-56899-623-3 (pbk.)
   1. Underground Railroad — Juvenile fiction. [1. Underground railroad—Fiction. 2. Fugitive
slaves—Fiction. 3. Slavery—Fiction. 4. Time travel—Fiction 5. Afro-Americans—Fiction.]
I. Velasquez, Eric, ill.   II. Title.   III. Series: Odyssey (Smithsonian Institution)
PZ7.G2414Es 1999   98-42567
[Fic]—dc21   CIP
                                                                                              AC

Escape!

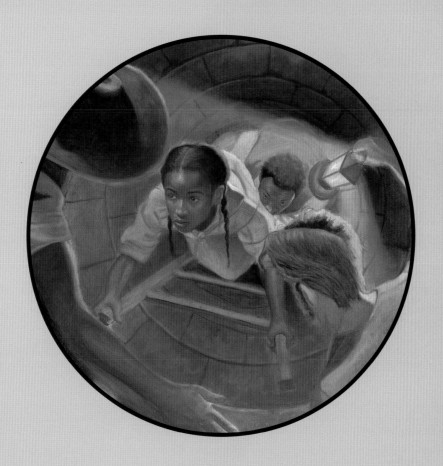

ODYSSEY

"Where's Emma?" asks Tomas as he, Kevin, and Lucy leave the Anacostia Museum. The museum is part of the Smithsonian Institution, and the friends have been looking at an exhibit called "Before Freedom Came," about African-American life in the South before the Civil War.

"I'm coming," Emma answers, walking slowly through the museum doors.

"Hey, hurry up!" says Tomas. "We're going on the trail next!"

"You guys go on. I'll catch up in a minute," says Emma softly.

"What's wrong?" Lucy asks. Emma doesn't seem as bouncy as when they came.

"Slavery was horrible!" exclaims Emma.

"I know," agrees Kevin. "It was good that people could escape on the Underground Railroad."

Emma follows her friends along the George Washington Carver Nature Trail, letting them walk ahead.

"Oh, there are some of Mama's favorite flowers!" Emma says to herself. "Maybe I'll make a sketch for her." Crawling over a log and lying on her stomach, she begins to sketch the delicate flowers.

"Emma!" a voice suddenly calls in a frantic whisper. "Where are you, Emma?"

"Here I am," says Emma, getting up and turning around. She is startled to notice that it is nearly dark. A thin girl is standing in front of her. She looks just a little older than Emma herself.

Before Emma can speak, the girl gathers her into a quick hug.

"Oh, sweet Emma, I got so scared when I couldn't find you! I'm glad you're safe!"

"What's happening?" Emma asks.

"It's time! We must go this minute," the girl says to Emma. "There may never be another chance to join your mother in Canada. Hitch up your dress. We have to run!"

Emma starts to say she's wearing pants, but looks down and sees she has on a long dress of rough material.

Suddenly the sound of barking dogs can be heard coming from the woods.

"Get down!" the girl whispers sharply. She drops to her hands and knees and begins to crawl quickly. "Master Herrot put the dogs on our trail! Stay low like me. We're almost to the wagon your Papa got. We've got to outrun those dogs!"

10

The two girls scramble over rocks and twigs with the dogs barking behind them. Just when Emma thinks she'll trip and fall, she hears the girl's frantic whisper. "There's the wagon! Stay close!"

It is now completely dark. Emma gropes to find the girl. Strong hands grab hers and pull her up in the air. Other hands push from behind. In the blink of an eye, Emma finds herself inside a wooden wagon.

"You all right, Sister-Ann?" a deep voice asks in the darkness.

"Yes, Ben-John, I'm fine." Emma recognizes the voice of the girl. "And Emma's all right too, Roland."

"Praise be!" says a different man's voice. "Emma, honey, get right down in the wagon so you can't be seen."

Emma lies flat, and two very small children snuggle next to her. The wagon begins to roll. After hours of bumping along, the wagon stops.

"All right, my girl," says Papa Roland. His strong hands lift her out of the wagon and, carrying Emma, he begins to walk very fast.

"Where are we?" Emma whispers.

"We've just crossed from Georgia into South Carolina. We've got to look for the man who's going to hide us," says Papa Roland, "our conductor on the Underground Railroad."

Emma gasps. The Underground Railroad! *We're escaping!* she realizes.

Ben-John and Sister-Ann each carry a small child. They are half-walking, half-running.

"Over here! Hurry—it's almost daylight!" A voice is calling to them from the darkness. An elderly white man in a nightshirt stands before them, holding a lantern beside a well. Next instant, Emma and the others are climbing down a rickety ladder deep into the old, dried-up well.

"Here are bread, cheese, and fruit," says the man, handing down a sack. Then he lowers a small pail filled with water. The old man pulls the ladder up. Emma hears him dragging it away. Then he pulls the well cover halfway across the top.

A rooster crows, and for a long time, nobody speaks.

"How did the man know we were coming?" Emma asks.

"He bought some farm equipment from our master," Papa Roland explains. "Master Herrot was sending it over in a wagon. His niece works for the Underground. When the master came out to inspect the wagon, she was with him. After he was satisfied and went back in, she gave one long and two short whistles. That told me that it was time to come hide in the wagon.

"Now we've got to find your mama!" Papa Roland adds, giving Emma a squeeze. "My Leah! I'm so proud of that gal escaping to the North all on her own!"

By now, Emma has figured out that Ben-John is Papa Roland's brother, that Sister-Ann is Ben-John's wife, and that they have four-year-old twins—a girl named Hester and a boy, DeVane.

As the sun gets higher it becomes stuffy in the dry, old well. Emma is too hot and drowsy to stand, so she slides to the ground. The men, too big to sit on the well floor, move their feet to make room for her and the twins.

"Here Emma, suck on this rag." Sister-Ann dips a small, gray rag into the pail and wrings it out. She dips another rag in the water for her children.

From above, Emma thinks she hears thunder, but then she realizes it's the sound of horses galloping.

"What's down there?" drawls a man's voice very near.

"That well has been out of use for years," says the old man's voice.

"Samuel! Move that cover. Let's have a look."

Emma holds her breath as the voices get louder. Then she hears the sound of dogs barking in the distance.

"The hounds have picked up a scent in the woods, Herrot," says another man's drawl.

"All right, leave the well be." Then, to the old man, "Just know, if those slaves turn up near your house, Sir, you'll have some mighty quick explaining to do!"

In the well, everyone breathes a sigh of relief. They are safe from the slave trackers—for now.

By night, the old man comes to help them out of the well. After hasty farewells, they begin to run. Just at sunrise, they come to another farm. This time they hide in a big haystack.

Days and nights go on in this way. They run at night, their only thought to reach the next station on the Underground Railroad. Sometimes the conductor is a man, sometimes a woman. To Emma's surprise, once it's a young girl her own age.

One night Papa Roland suddenly stops in front of a carved stone that is sticking out of the ground. He falls to his knees and puts his arms around the stone.

"Roland, are you sick?" asks Sister-Ann.

"No, not sick!" he exclaims. "We just crossed the Mason-Dixon line!"

"The border between Maryland and Pennsylvania," Emma says. "We're in the North!"

They all laugh and dance for joy in the moonlight, but Papa Roland soon quiets them, saying, "We can't stop running, though—not till we cross to Canada!"

Through mountain passes and deep woods they travel, guided by secret signs they've been told to look for. Soon they see a farm up ahead. Emma hopes it's their next station. Suddenly, the farmhouse door opens and out steps a smiling Black couple.

"Welcome! Come in, come in!"

Emma looks at Sister-Ann. "We're going in their house?"

Sister-Ann nods happily. In all their travels they had never entered someone's home. For the first time since this all began, Emma feels she can let down her guard.

"I'm Edwina, and that's my husband, Daniel," says the woman, handing Emma and the others small piles of clean clothes. She pushes aside a chair and lifts a trapdoor, leading them down narrow stairs to a large, clean room. In the room are a table, chairs, and several beds.

Emma sits on one of the beds. She sniffs the good smell of clean sheets and clothes. The twins watch her and, giggling, sniff their clothes, too. Sister-Ann and Edwina pull out a large tub, then fill it with kettles of warm water. First the twins are washed, then Emma gets a bath. Emma barely crawls in with the twins before she is fast asleep.

Later, the others talk and make plans. Edwina tells them she has always been free, and that her parents left her the farm.

"One night, Daniel walked out of the shadows, and told me he was a runaway slave," says Edwina. "He looked so brave and strong, I fell in love right then! We've been helping runaways ever since."

"What about your children?" asks Sister-Ann.

Edwina shakes her head, but a gentle smile comes over her face.

"Daniel and I say that every slave we help escape is one of our children."

For several days they stay in the large room, only venturing out at night. Even then, the children can't play and run free—in case anyone is watching. After a few days, Daniel comes home with news.

"I got the song today! I was out working my mules when a tinker came by. He was singing about Leah being up high in the beautiful country. So, your wife is all right!"

"It's time for the rest of our journey," beams Papa Roland.

"The man also sang of slave trackers in the area," Daniel adds seriously. "I think it's safer not to use the wagon. Better go on foot, and leave tonight."

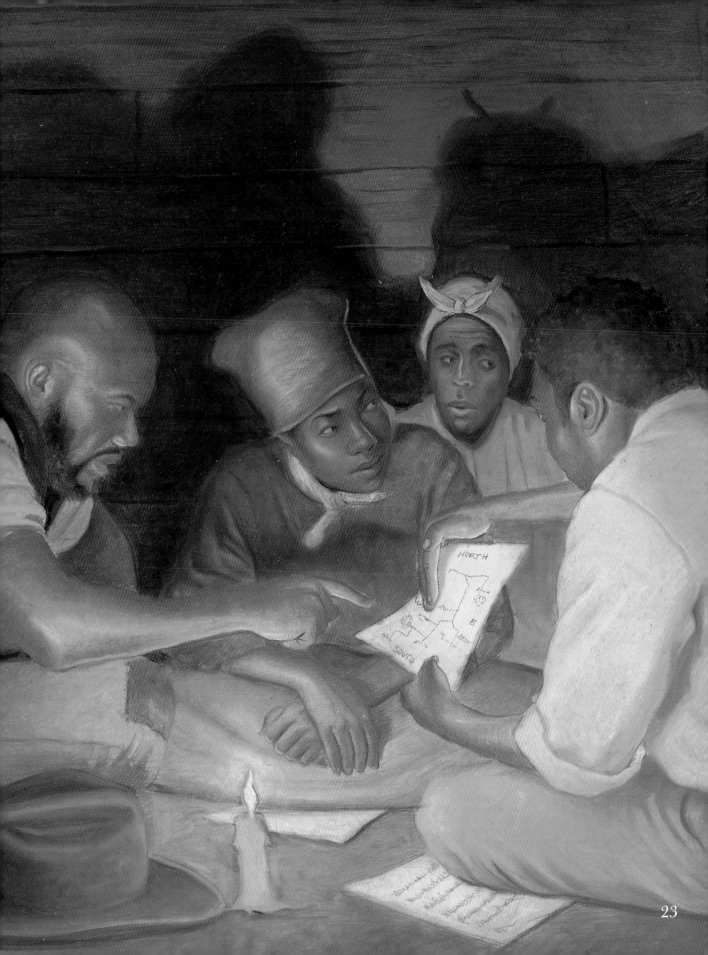

23

When it's fully dark, Edwina gives them small pouches of food. Peeking in, Emma sees cornbread, bacon, and some dried fruit. Outside, they all turn for a last look at the house. Edwina and Daniel embrace them.

"Now, run!" says Daniel in a low voice.

Again, they run and run and run.

"Hold on to my neck, Emma," says Papa Roland, picking her up. "We're nearing the border of Canada, but we can't stop to rest now."

Close to daylight, Papa Roland slows. "Get down!" he calls out. They all drop and lie flat on their stomachs. Emma's heart is pounding so loud, it sounds like horses galloping. After a while it quiets, and Emma listens to insect sounds in the tall grass. It gets very hot, and she lifts her head to wipe her face.

"Keep your head down, Emma!" Papa Roland whispers.

After a time, she hears twigs snap. "Papa Roland, is that you?" Emma whispers. There is no answer.

Finally, it begins to grow dark. "You can sit up now, honey," murmurs Sister-Ann. "You should eat something now, too."

Emma sits up stiffly. "Where are Papa Roland and Uncle Ben-John?" she asks.

"They're waiting for us at the river. Now hurry, eat your food," whispers Sister-Ann, turning her attention to the twins.

When they finish eating, Sister-Ann motions Emma to follow. She lifts DeVane and starts to walk. Emma picks up Hester and follows close behind.

They reach the river, and Papa Roland helps them into a rowboat. Emma leans against Sister-Ann. The boat rocks back and forth. It's cool, and Emma is lulled by the sound of the oars dipping carefully in and out of the water.

"Emma! Emma, wake up! You're free!" Sister-Ann shouts at the top of her lungs. Emma sits bolt upright and rubs her eyes. *Free!* Emma has never heard a word sound so glorious in all her life.

"My baby! My baby," a slender woman with tears of joy running down her cheeks showers Emma with kisses. Papa Roland wraps both of them in his big strong arms and they all hug and hug. Emma wishes this moment could last forever.

"Leah?" Papa Roland asks in a booming voice. It is the first time Emma has heard him speak aloud. "Leah, first thing tomorrow we're going, in plain sight, to the top of the highest hill we can find, and drink and eat as much freedom as the Lord will allow!"

"Amen!" they all shout. Everyone is laughing and hugging and dancing. Emma twirls round and round until she's too dizzy to stand.

"Why were you twirling around like that, Emma?" asks Tomas.

Emma stops and looks around. Everything seems bright and clear and—free! Emma gasps, realizing Tomas, Lucy, and Kevin are staring at her. She looks around, spotting her pencils and pad, with the sketch of her mother's favorite flowers.

"Where were you? We've been looking everywhere!" announces Kevin.

"Oh! I saw some pretty flowers behind that log. I stopped to sketch them," says Emma, gathering up her things and holding them close. "Did I miss much?"

"Well, there was a trail through the woods, just like the runaways used on the Underground Railroad," says Lucy. "I'll go back with you if you want to see it."

"That's okay," says Emma, smiling. "I think I've already seen enough trails!"

"You sure?" says Lucy.

"I'm very sure!" answers Emma.

About the Underground Railroad

The Underground Railroad was a network of safe places that helped enslaved Black people in the southern part of the United States to escape. Between 1830 and 1865, when the Civil War ended, it is believed that about one hundred thousand slaves traveled on the Underground Railroad.

The Underground Railroad was not a real railroad. It was made up of paths, stops, and landmarks which began in the South, ran through the North, and ended in Canada. The Mason-Dixon line, the border between Maryland and Pennsylvania, separated the slave-owning states of the South from the North, where most people did not own slaves.

The people who escaped were called runaways or fugitives. The Fugitive Slave Act, passed in 1793, allowed slaveholders to bring runaways to court so that they could reclaim them. Since slaves were thought of as property, many people made a living by capturing runaways and taking them back to their owners. They were paid for every slave they returned. Because of this, runaways had to keep running even after they crossed the Mason-Dixon line into the North. They had to keep going into Canada, where they could not be recaptured.

Runaways, or "passengers" on the Underground Railroad, usually traveled at night. They followed the North Star to keep them on course, and relied on the "railways" of secretly-marked paths, back roads, fields, and tunnels. Many traveled on rivers, streams, and other waterways, because no footprints were left behind and bloodhounds could not follow the scent. During the day, runaways hid in safe "stations" such as barn lofts, haystacks, as well as secret rooms in houses or churches.

Free people, both black and white, who risked their lives to help slaves escape were known as "conductors" or "stationmasters." Some brought runaways from one station to another. Others planned escapes and told slaves when travel was safe. They left signs, such as a candle in a certain window, or a lantern in the front yard. Directions and secret codes were also hidden in the words of songs, especially spirituals.

One of the most famous conductors of the Underground Railroad was Harriet Tubman. In 1849, she escaped from Maryland, made 19 trips to the South, and helped deliver thousands of people to freedom.

Even though the Underground Railroad was a secret operation, its dramatic story was kept alive even after slavery ended. Abolitionists—people who opposed slavery—fought against slavery without using violence. The Underground Railroad will always be remembered as a movement that worked to stop the mistreatment of human beings.

Glossary

abolitionist: Someone who was strongly against slavery.

conductor: An individual who risked his or her life to take slaves from station to station on the Underground Railroad.

"get the sign" or *"get the song":* To receive coded messages from the Underground Railroad about "safe" places, where one could get food or shelter.

Mason-Dixon line: The border between Maryland and Pennsylvania, surveyed by Charles Mason and Jeremiah Dixon in 1760, marked by carved milestones. It became the dividing line between the slave-owning South and the North, where most people did not own slaves.

North Star: A star used as a beacon in the night sky to let runaways know they were headed in the right direction—north to freedom. The North Star is also called Polaris, and is part of the constellation Ursa Minor.

safe house: A place—usually a secret room, an attic, or a cellar—where runaway slaves hid for safety.

slave trackers: Anti-abolitionists who followed and tried to catch runaways, often using bloodhounds, with the hope of getting reward money.

station: A rest stop where escaping slaves received food, shelter, and money. The stations were usually about ten to thirty miles apart.

stationmaster: The owner of a free house or station.

Underground Railroad: A network of people and places set up to help slaves escape to freedom between 1830 and 1865. This network extended from the South to the northern part of the United States and up into Canada.